ZORA NEALE HURSTON

POWER
OF THE PEN

BLACK
WOMEN
WRITERS

T0062006

by Joyce Markovics

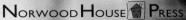

NORWOOD HOUSE PRESS

NORWOOD HOUSE PRESS

For more information about Norwood House Press, please visit our website at:
www.norwoodhousepress.com or call 866-565-2900.

Book Designer: Ed Morgan
Editorial and Production: Bowerbird Books

Photo Credits: Library of Congress, cover and title page; State Library and Archives of Florida, 5; © Everett Collection/Newscom, 6; The New York Public Library, 7; State Library and Archives of Florida, 8; Wikimedia Commons, 9; Wikimedia Commons/Farm Security Administration, 10; Wikimedia Commons, 11; Library of Congress, 12; Wikimedia Commons/Emma Langdon Roche, 13; freepik.com, 14; Library of Congress, 15; © spatuletail/Shutterstock, 16; © St Petersburg Times/ZUMAPRESS/Newscom, 17; State Library and Archives of Florida, 18; State Library and Archives of Florida, 19; Library of Congress, 21.

Library of Congress Cataloging-in-Publication Data

Names: Markovics, Joyce L., author.
Title: Zora Neale Hurston / by Joyce Markovics.
Description: Buffalo : Norwood House Press, 2024. | Series: Power of the
   pen: Black women writers | Includes bibliographical references and
   index. | Audience: Grades 4-6
Identifiers: LCCN 2023045977 (print) | LCCN 2023045978 (ebook) | ISBN
   9781684506729 (hardcover) | ISBN 9781684049738 (paperback) | ISBN
   9781684049790 (ebook)
Subjects: LCSH: Hurston, Zora Neale--Juvenile literature. | Authors,
   American--20th century--Biography--Juvenile literature. | African
   American authors--Biography--Juvenile literature. | African American
   women--Biography--Juvenile literature. | African American women
   authors--Biography--Juvenile literature. | Folklorists--United
   States--Biography--Juvenile literature. | LCGFT: Biographies. | Picture
   books.
Classification: LCC PS3515.U789 Z7825 2024 (print) | LCC PS3515.U789
   (ebook) | DDC 813/.54 [B]--dc23/eng/20231003
LC record available at https://lccn.loc.gov/2023045977
LC ebook record available at https://lccn.loc.gov/2023045978

372N--012024

Manufactured in the United States of America in North Mankato, Minnesota.

CONTENTS

INTRODUCING ZORA

"If you haven't got it, you can't show it. If you have got it, you can't hide it."

Zora Neale Hurston was a collector of stories. She gathered them like precious flowers. Her focus was African American people. She loved Black **culture** and became an expert on **folklore**. She wrote novels based on her experiences and research. Her most famous book was *Their Eyes Were Watching God*. During her life, Zora got little praise for her **innovative** work. But she didn't let other people define her. She defined herself!

ASK YOURSELF
WHY IS IT IMPORTANT TO COLLECT OTHER PEOPLE'S STORIES?

Zora Neale Hurston was endlessly curious about Black life.

ZORA WAS AN **ANTHROPOLOGIST** AND A WRITER. SHE WAS A TEACHER TOO. SHE TAUGHT DRAMA TO BLACK STUDENTS.

EARLY YEARS

In January 1891, Zora Neale Lee Hurston was born in Notasulga, Alabama. Her parents were John and Lucy. They had eight children, including Zora. John was a **sharecropper** and carpenter. He later became a preacher. Zora and her strict father were often at odds. She didn't follow his rules. Her constant questions annoyed him. However, Zora's mom encouraged her curious daughter. Lucy wanted her children to be bold and "jump at the sun," said Zora.

Zora as a young person in the South

When Zora was a toddler, her family moved to Eatonville, Florida. It was one of a few all-Black towns in the United States. There, Zora's family lived in a big house. Her dad became mayor. Zora described Eatonville as "the center of the world." It would become an important part of her. She often visited the general store to hear people swap stories. Those tales would "hang in my ear," Zora said.

For the most part, Black people could live freely in Eatonville. Zora often said she was born there.

EVERYTHING IN EATONVILLE WAS RUN BY BLACK PEOPLE, INCLUDING THE GOVERNMENT. IN OTHER PARTS OF FLORIDA, WHITE PEOPLE WERE IN CONTROL. AND **RACISM** WAS WIDESPREAD.

> **There is no agony like bearing an untold story inside you.**

When Zora was 13, her mother got sick and died. In an instant, Zora's world flipped. "That moment was the end of a phase of life for me," she said. It was also when Zora's family was together "for the last time on earth." Her father quickly remarried. He sent Zora to live with her older siblings in Jacksonville, Florida. Once there, Zora felt adrift and alone. She missed Eatonville with all her heart.

A portrait of Zora in Eatonville

ASK YOURSELF
CAN YOU THINK OF A SAD TIME IN YOUR LIFE? DOES IT STILL AFFECT YOU?

For a short time, Zora went to school in Jacksonville. Then her father stopped paying her **tuition**. Zora had to scrub the schools' floors to finish out the year. After that, Zora was fully on her own. She called this time her "haunted years." "I was shifted from house to house . . . and found comfort nowhere," said Zora.

Jacksonville, Florida, in the 1900s

> **No job, no friends, and a lot of hope.**

For the next eight years, Zora tried her best to support herself. "I wanted books and school," she said. But these things were far away. "I would cry inside," said Zora. When she turned 26, Zora moved to Baltimore, Maryland. She worked as a waitress, maid, and **manicurist**. But she still craved an education. So, she **enrolled** herself in night school.

It was next to impossible for Black women to find good-paying jobs in the early 1900s. Many, like Zora, worked as maids for white families.

A gifted student, Zora graduated in 1918. The next year, she went to Howard University in Washington, DC. Zora helped found the school's first newspaper. She also began writing short stories. In 1925, she **published** "Spunk." That same year, Zora got a scholarship to Barnard College in Harlem, New York. She studied anthropology with Franz Boas. He believed no culture was better than another. Zora agreed. Three years later, Zora got an anthropology degree—and a new focus.

These are early graduates of Barnard College. The college was founded by women in 1889 after nearby Columbia University wouldn't admit them.

ZORA WAS THE FIRST BLACK WOMAN TO GRADUATE FROM BARNARD COLLEGE. SHE FACED RACISM FROM TEACHERS AND STUDENTS. SO, ZORA LIVED OFF CAMPUS IN A BLACK COMMUNITY.

HER WORK

Zora playing a drum

Zora was living in Harlem during an exciting time. There was an explosion of Black art and pride. It was called the **Harlem Renaissance**. Zora's home became a meeting place for Black artists. She got to know the writers Langston Hughes and Countee Cullen. Together, they created *Fire!!*, a Black **literary** magazine. Zora wrote short stories and a play for the magazine.

THE HARLEM RENAISSANCE TOOK PLACE DURING THE 1920S AND 1930S. IT WAS A MOVEMENT THAT CELEBRATED BLACK ARTISTS. IT ALSO BROUGHT ATTENTION TO BLACK AMERICANS' FIGHT FOR EQUAL RIGHTS.

In 1927, Zora traveled south to study Black culture. She spoke to Cudjoe Lewis in Alabama. At the time, he was one of the last survivors of the **Atlantic slave trade**. Zora recorded his moving story. She described Cudjoe as "the only man on earth who has in his heart the memory of his African home."

Zora then interviewed Black people all over the South. She learned their folklore, music, and dance. Zora called her research "poking and prying with a purpose." All the while, seeds for books were growing in her mind.

Cudjoe Lewis was thought to originally have been from Benin, Africa. He was captured and enslaved when he was a young man.

> "I have been in Sorrow's kitchen and licked out all the pots. Then I have stood on the peaky mountain wrapped in rainbows, with a harp and a sword in my hands."
>
> –*Jonah's Gourd Vine*

In 1929, Zora settled in Florida and wrote. She published the novel *Jonah's Gourd Vine* in 1934. It was based on her childhood in Eatonville. In the book, Zora included the local speech, or **vernacular**, of her youth. She wove in Black folklore too. **Critics** praised the book. Though Zora earned little money from her book sales.

Zora found beauty and inspiration in mountains like these.

ZORA LOVED NATURE. IT INSPIRED HER WRITING. "I WAS ONLY HAPPY IN THE WOODS." SHE ALSO LIKED IT WHEN THE "SPRINGTIME CAME STROLLING FROM THE SEA."

In 1935, Zora published another book. *Mules and Men* was a collection of Black folklore. Nothing like it had ever been written. Yet many anthropologists didn't take her work seriously. Zora then worked with Langston Hughes to make the book into a play. Their effort failed—as did their once close friendship. Zora still wanted to see her work on stage. She created a Broadway show called *The Great Day*. It had positive reviews. Yet it closed after only one performance.

Born in 1901, Langston Hughes was an important Black writer and leader.

ASK YOURSELF
THINK ABOUT A TIME WHEN YOU FAILED AT SOMETHING. HOW DO YOU THINK FAILURES CAN LEAD TO SUCCESSES?

There are years that ask questions and years that answer." –*Their Eyes Were Watching God*

In 1937, Zora got a research **grant**. She went to Haiti and Jamaica. In Haiti, she wrote *Their Eyes Were Watching God*. She finished it in just seven weeks. The novel was "dammed up in me," said Zora. The story follows Janie Crawford, a driven Black woman much like Zora. At that time, few books centered on Black women. In her novel, Zora discussed race, culture, and love. The book was a rich portrait of Black life.

A postage stamp featuring Zora from 2003.

When the book was published, reviews were mixed. Black and white critics attacked it. Some said it was insulting to Black people. However, others saw the novel's warmth, humor, and sadness. Ignoring her critics, Zora kept publishing books. "If writers were too wise, perhaps no books would get written at all," she later said.

Zora in Florida

IN THE 1930S, ZORA STARTED A DRAMA SCHOOL AT BETHUNE-COOKMAN COLLEGE IN DAYTONA BEACH, FLORIDA. SHE LATER WORKED AS A DRAMA TEACHER.

> **Grab the broom of anger and drive off the beast of fear.**

Despite some writing success, Zora struggled to get by. She went on research trips when she could. To pay her bills, she worked as a **freelancer**. She covered the story of a Black woman charged with killing a white doctor. Because of a dispute about her pay, Zora left the assignment. From then on, she worked odd jobs. In 1957, she was fired from one job for being "too well-educated." A **dispirited** Zora found work as a maid. She took the job just to "live a little."

ASK YOURSELF
WHAT DO YOU THINK THE MEASURE OF SUCCESS IS? IS IT MONEY OR FAME—OR SOMETHING ELSE ALTOGETHER?

Zora (left) on a research trip

Zora's health began to decline. Poor and sick, she moved to the St. Lucie County **Welfare** Home in Florida. She wrote, "If I do happen to die without money, somebody will bury me, though I do not wish it to be that way." On January 28, 1960, Zora Neale Hurston died penniless. She was buried in an unmarked grave. Sadly, Zora found little **acclaim** during her life. Thankfully, that would soon change.

It's believed Zora died from heart disease.

ONE OF ZORA'S LAST TEACHING JOBS WAS AT LINCOLN PARK ACADEMY IN FORT PIECE, FLORIDA. THERE, SHE TAUGHT ENGLISH.

ZORA'S POWER

A thing is mighty big when time and distance cannot shrink it.

Today, Zora is viewed as a leading anthropologist and writer. Her books have sold millions of copies. They've inspired other Black women writers, including Zadie Smith and Alice Walker. When Zadie first read *Their Eyes Were Watching God* at age 14, she was in awe. The book "had me pinned to the ground, unable to deny its strength," she said. Alice grew up not knowing Zora's work—or that of any other Black women writers. When Alice discovered Zora's books, she was hooked. Alice found Zora's unmarked grave. In 1972, she bought her a headstone. And Alice spread the word about Zora's incredible talents. "A people do not throw their geniuses away," Alice said. Zora's powerful impact continues to grow.

ZORA'S BOOK ABOUT CUDJOE LEWIS, *BARRACOON*, WAS FINALLY PUBLISHED IN 2018.

Zora once wrote, "I will remember you all in my good thoughts, and I ask you kindly to do the same for me."

ASK YOURSELF
HOW DO YOU WANT TO BE REMEMBERED?

TIMELINE AND ACTIVITY

January 1891
Zora is born in Notasulga, Alabama

1894
Zora's family moves to Eatonville, Florida

1904
Lucy, Zora's mother, dies

1919
Zora attends Howard University

1925
Zora goes to Barnard College and gets a degree in anthropology

1934–1935
Zora publishes her first and second books, *Jonah's Gourd Vine* and *Mules and Men*

1937
Their Eyes Were Watching God is published

January 28, 1960
Zora dies at age 69

GET WRITING!

Zora Neale Hurston was a scientist and storyteller who combined her passions. Think of two different things you love. Write a short story about both of them. Share your work with an adult or friend!

GLOSSARY

acclaim (uh-KLEYM): public praise.

anthropologist (an-thruh-POL-uh-jist): a scientist who studies people and their cultures.

Atlantic slave trade (at-LAN-tik SLEYV TREYD): the transportation of millions of enslaved Africans across the Atlantic Ocean to the Americas from the 1600 to 1800s.

critics (KRIT-iks): people who judge or criticize something.

culture (KUHL-chur): the customs and traditions shared by a group of people.

dispirited (dih-SPIR-ih-tid): hopeless.

enrolled (en-ROHLD): registered for something.

folklore (FOHK-lor): the stories and beliefs of a group of people.

freelancer (FREE-lans-uhr): a person who works for different companies at different times.

grant (GRANT): money given by a group to a person for a special purpose.

Harlem Renaissance (HAHR-luhm REN-uh-sans): an art movement in Harlem, New York, during the 1920s and 1930s.

innovative (in-uh-VAY-tiv): having new ideas about how something can be done.

literary (LIT-uh-rer-see): concerning writing and the study of written works.

manicurist (MAN-ih-kyoor-ist): a person who trims and paints fingernails.

published (PUHB-lishd): printed or made available for people to read.

racism (REY-siz-uhm): a system of beliefs and policies based on the idea that one race is better than another.

sharecropper (SHAIR-krop-er): a farmer who gives a part of each crop as rent.

tuition (too-ISH-uhn): money charged to attend a school.

vernacular (ver-NAK-yuh-ler): the common language of a place.

welfare (WEL-fair): refers to caring for people in need.

FOR MORE INFORMATION

Books

Hurston, Zora Neale. *Lies and Other Tall Tales*. New York, NY: HarperCollins, 2005.
Read stories collected by Zora Neale Hurston.

Hurston, Zora Neale. *The Making of Butterflies*. New York, NY: Amistad Books, 2023.
Zora Neale Hurston introduces readers to folklore about the origin of butterflies.

O'Neill, Bill. *The Great Book of Black Heroes*. Sheridan, WY: LAK Publishing, 2021.
Explore the lives of 30 incredible Black people.

Websites

Britannica Kids: Zora Neale Hurston
(https://kids.britannica.com/students/article/Zora-Neale-Hurston/311769)
Learn about Zora Neale Hurston's life.

The Official Website of Zora Neale Hurston
(https://www.zoranealehurston.com)
Discover more about who Zora Neale Hurston was.

INDEX

ABOUT THE AUTHOR

Joyce Markovics has written hundreds of children's books. She's passionate about celebrating the lives and accomplishments of women. Joyce dedicates this book to Joyce Sharrock Cole, a super woman.

POWER OF THE PEN

BLACK WOMEN WRITERS

ZORA NEALE HURSTON

Zora Neale Hurston was a pioneering anthropologist and writer. With her pen, she told powerful stories. She and other Black women writers raise their voices to describe the experiences of Black Americans. In the process, they have helped shape American literature and culture—and reached millions of readers!

Scan here to see a complete list of titles included in this series.

ISBN: 978-1-68404-973-8

NORWOOD HOUSE  PRESS

9 781684 049738